# New Beginnings

By Ashleigh Aynn Willhite

# ACKNOWLEDGEMENTS

I thank the Holy Spirit for taking me on all these adventures, my parents and husband for their constant support, and for every person who welcomed me in on their journey with them.

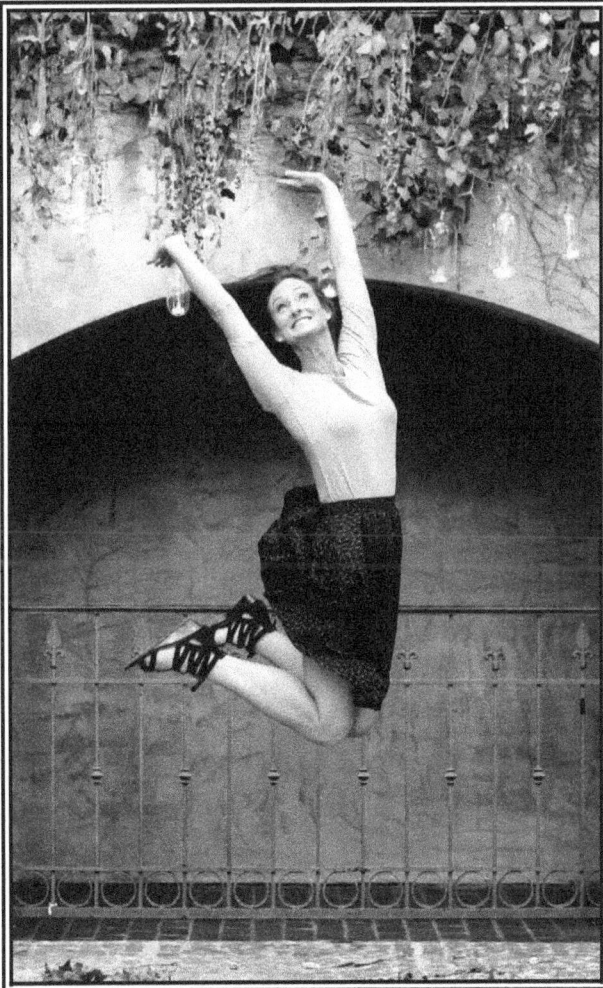

Ashleigh Aynn Willhite

# CONTENTS

# Introduction

Whether you are reading this because you are bored, getting the internal nudge to be quiet and re-evaluate your life, wanting some inspiration, or a friend recommended it to you, I hope and pray you enjoy reading my stories. This short book gives an account of a few significant parts of my actual life, told as I remember, from a contemplative perspective. Stories of pain, adventure, learning, business, marriage, travel, and of my relationship with God.

I originally wrote this book for prison inmates. I was once in jail for a period of time. That is where I learned to talk to God, hear from God, and pray. I had the time. It was the greatest blessing. But it wasn't just for me. I was learning how to effectively and powerfully pray on behalf of others. When I got out of jail and a year later began volunteering in that same jail, I wanted the inmates to also see how much they were loved and forgiven, as well as feel that same sense of purpose I had felt. I sought to help them understand that while they were cut off from society, their prayers were not. I thought this book would be a part of my dream for them. But shortly before publishing this, I felt the direction change.

While God does want to teach inmates how to pray, there were many others that He wanted to reach. People who sincerely wanted to include God in every aspect of their life but didn't know how. People who didn't know they needed to include God. People who needed a fresh start. People who were looking for a New Beginning.

As I sit in my house with my husband and child during this Covid-10 quarantine, my heart sighs a sigh of relief. And my spirit is full of anticipation and hope. It is not easy to go through difficult times, even when you do have great faith. From a human perspective, this economic and health crisis is terrible, but perhaps God is wanting to connect with us. Perhaps He doesn't want things to go back to "normal." Perhaps He has some things to show us. I imagine some of those things will cause us to face changes we need to make, but I think most of what He wants to show us is how loving He is and how much we can't...and don't...want to live without Him...or without others.

What if thousands of us have been living the dream, achieving everything we set out to achieve, and never realize how far away we are from God? Or what if we have been desperately desiring to slow down and connect with Him, but cannot seem to find the time, no matter how hard we try? Maybe now is the time. Maybe now it is time to take the time to "figure it out." Figure out how to connect with God and find out His will for every area of your life. Or if that seems impossible, at least experience hope deep within you that will strengthen you to keep moving forward in the right direction, no matter how difficult it seems. Cheers to a New Beginning! Anything is possible if you believe. Enjoy reading!

# *1*

# *Childhood Dreams*

I was not raised in a Christian home. My parents are amazing. I just don't remember hearing anything about God and we didn't go to church. If my parents talked about God or spirituality, I don't remember hearing it. So, the dreams I had as a small child could not have been from anything I was taught or heard about from other people. It had to come from another reality that I would not be consciously aware of until years later.

I don't know my exact age, maybe 3, maybe 6, I have no idea, but as a small child, I had a reoccurring dream of angels and demons. For years I dreamt this dream in black and white. For some reason, I never told my parents. (This would be a pattern of mine in my teenage years, keeping deep things inside, hidden.) I dreamt of these small black demons that were not very tall, maybe 2 feet in height. I was walking in a straight line and on both side of me they were lined up, reaching out to terrify me. I don't remember any noise, just the terrifying appearance of these black evil things that were intentionally scaring me. They were all looking right at me, waving their arms and moving chaotically about. I was so afraid. I crouched down low and squeezed my eyes closed and just wanted to keep walking and make it through

And suddenly, the scene would change. Those black demons disappeared and now appeared super tall, like 8 feet tall angels. They were light in color, a shade of white. They were graceful and seemed to move very slowly. If you can imagine a sloth dancing, that's about the slowness of their dancing and waving gently back and forth. I felt so safe. Protected. I stood up tall and walked on my tippy toes, stretching my arms out wide. I was happy and peaceful and safe. My heart felt light and free. It was wonderful.

And then I woke up.

I didn't consciously start pondering on this dream until I became a Christian, which was many years later. This dream depicted the first decade of my walk with the Lord. I struggled back and forth between fear (caused by the enemy) and freedom and courage that God often brought through His Spirit and His angels.

Recently, I had a vision that brought so much redemption to the years of torment I walked in. In the vision, I saw the same demons and angels, but this time, the huge angels were lined up on both sides of me and the demons were on the outside of the angels. They couldn't touch me. God's Psalm 91 protection was surrounding me and the enemy had to get through them to get to me, which wasn't happening. We are in a spiritual battle, to which I am grateful that the

Lord has already fought and won on our behalf.

# 2

## *AS A YOUNG PERSON*

I made all A's in school My mom read to me from a young age and had me doing school work from the age of 3. While I was an only child, I had many friends. Mom drove 35 minutes one way to take me to gymnastics practice. I loved that sport. We stretched for sometimes over an hour. One time we stretched in front of a mirror and learned how to roll our tongues. I got up to three rolls and, to this day, can still make my tongue go into that weird shape! Dad worked hard to provide all of our needs and many wants. He built me an incredible playgound, including two playhouses! We had a boat and went to Lake Santa Fe frequently. I especially loved to go tubing and glaze over the smooth glass looking water, clutching the handles as tight as I could until Dad whipped around and threw me off. My entire family, grandparents, aunts, uncles, and cousins lived up north. It was a 15-hour drive or a 3-hour plane ride, but we visited both sides at least twice a year. Christmas at my grandparents' house was my favorite. And then Turkey Run. This beautiful state park that had the funnest nature trails with a swinging bride that went over the creek. We often met the other side of the family there (and years later I actually got married there). I had the sweetest childhood. I was a social butterfly and my parents taught me that I could do anything I wanted to do. I had a lot of fun growing up and I truly believed that anything was possible. And then my teenage years hit. They hit me hard. My hormones were really out of whack. I had such severe PMS that I thought of killing myself at times. I distinctly remember grabbing a steak knife, running to my closet, crouching down in a ball, and staring at my wrists with an intense, painful desire to end my life. This was one of those things that I kept hidden. It never occurred to me to talk to anyone about it. I loved to have fun as a kid and seemed to have a free spirit, and yet I didn't trust most people enough to let them see the real me, even my own parents I guess. With teenage insecurities and emotional pain, I sought out new friends. I wanted to hang out with the older, popular kids. And I did. When I was 14 I asked to hang out with a 16-year-old. I will never forget my first drinking party. I felt so cool. I felt like someone. And the alcohol? It was like a dream! It relieved all my anxiety, insecurities, and pain. I loved it. And I couldn't wait to do it again. I was lying to my parents in order to go to these parties and always pushing the envelope about how late I could stay out. The friction between my mom and I increased and we began fighting all the time. It was bad. She doesn't remember it being that bad. Maybe my memories of it was distorted. I don't know. But I'm sure the devil used every bit of it to drive a wedge and cause more pain. One day, in the 8th grade, a friend handed me a little blue pill. Actually, she gave me two. I asked her what it was. I don't remember if she told me, but I took it. About 20 minutes later, I was sitting in my English class and I started feeling light. Like completely relaxed. I loved it but I was also freaking out on the inside. I felt like my motor skills were slowing down so much that I didn't know if I would be able to speak clearly. But no one noticed. I was worried that it would comatose me or something but it didn't. I ended up feeling so good. And I started looking for that girl in the hallways more, craving those little pills. One day, my dad announced that he wasn't happy with mom anymore. I rarely saw them affectionate with each other, but they never fought. Mom yelled and dad withdrew; that was their pattern, but I never saw them give me any reason to be concerned for their marriage. Like, divorce never entered into my mind, even when dad said he wasn't happy. But, one week later, he left. I was sitting on the couch as dad was taking his suitcases out of the house. It was official, final. I was crying my eyes out, confused and wondering why. I kept asking why. It was hard for him, but he said he had to leave. I loved my dad so much. I held him up high on a pedestal; I think a lot of little girls see their dads as larger than life. A marriage and a divorce always takes two people and it's never one person's fault. I didn't see that at the time, but now I do. At the time, I rationalized that at least I still had both of my parents. Some people don't. At least I still had both and they both loved me. At least they were still around. That made sense to me and gave me no real reason to be overly emotional about it, although I was. I actually couldn't believe how painful it really was, but they were my world. As an only child with no other family around, it was tragic. It seemed to split me in two. Counseling, therapy, none of that came up as an option. Minimizing it through rationalization was the only way I knew how to cope with it. Anyway, after dad left, my view of men drastically changed. I put a huge wall of protection up and made a vow deep within my heart: "FORGET MEN! I DON'T NEED THEM IN MY LIFE!" When I got back home, I went totally numb. My mom said it was like a switch that just got turned off inside me. She tried to talk to me, reach me, but with a cold stare I looked at her and said, "If I am going to make it through high school, I need to deal with this how I deal with it." And that's when my alcohol and occasional drug usage went into a full-blown addiction. The high was constantly on my mind. I don't remember if my friends attempted to talk to me about my choices and behavior, but I found out years later that they were very worried and prayed for my life.

Mom and I

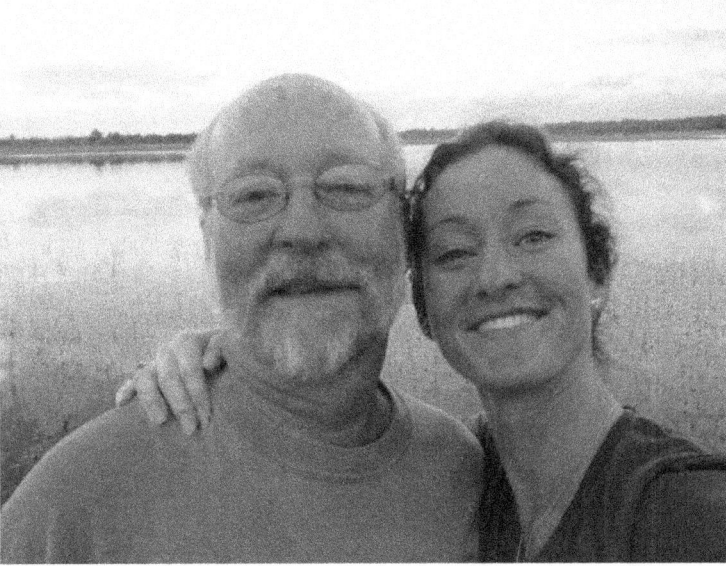

Dad and I

# 3

## *Darkness to Light*

Until my teenage years, I really did have the sweetest childhood. I was very blessed. Except the small town I grew up in had very little cultural diversity. I was naive to what I didn't know about, which included the street life. I'm embarrassed to say this because I have many friends of various races and cultures now, but my first experiences with African Americans were on the streets. There were only two that I remember in my K-12 grade school. My new black friends were the drug dealers. And that's what I thought that most black people did. I just didn't know any better. My parents weren't prejudice and had many friends of all socioeconomic backgrounds and ethnicities, but I did not. I don't think I was racist, but it was something I had to work through. I had to face the fact that my view of black people was extremely distorted. I believe we all have various prejudices based on our experiences and we really do need to be honest with ourselves and make the changes necessary. Anyway, let's get on with the story.

Although I graduated high school with an academic scholarship, I was a drug addict. I sought it out daily and lived for the high. The escape. The adventurous feeling of sneaking around and living life on the edge. I was this gangsta chic with power. I like the power. I felt like I had the status of a bad ass girl. It gave me a sense of confidence. A toughness that I needed in order to survive. And the drugs numbed out my pain and anxiety.

I became very reckless and manipulative. I totaled 5 or 6 cars from the age of 16 to 18 and didn't get hurt or a ticket in any of them. I deserved a "C" in some classes but often talked my way back up into an "A." I had a mini stroke from ecstasy, frequently drove high, and blindly went anywhere and stayed with anyone. I lied to my parents and was completely wrapped up in this dark life. I had no future plans of success. No one besides my mom sat down to talk with me about where my life was headed, at least from what I remember.

I didn't have sex with anyone before the drugs and street life came into the picture. I liked this one boy in the 5th grade. I think he called me one time on the phone but I was too nervous to talk. And around 16 I had a secret attraction for these two girls who I think kissed each other sometimes. That was it. I had no dating experience or any real friendship with any men. I mean, sure there were guys around, but nothing past a surface level. My first "experiences" were drug related. I was manipulated into doing "things" in exchange for the drugs. Somehow, with a sick feeling in my stomach and alarms going off in my mind trying to tell me NO!, I rationalized it wasn't a big deal and said, "Okay, I'll do it." I gave into the pressure and didn't listen to common sense or my own conscious. It was almost as if I didn't have an ability to say no to. Like, I really, really wanted to say no, but I couldn't. (My teenage rebellious years ruined my conscious. The more I defied the rules and boundaries, the harder it was to follow my conscious and make good choices). This led to many, many experiences of feeling like I was being raped. I actually was raped and told myself, "Well, you shouldn't have put yourself in that place." I went from every reason to hope, every reason to believe for a great future, to barely feeling human. Life? What life? I was full of shame, hated myself, and wanted to die. In fact, my secret prayer was, "God, if You exist, just take my life. Kill me." And He did in a way.

My *New Beginning* was when I realized that God existed. April of 2003 I was driving back from probation, considering smashing into the trees just to end it all. I was in a horrible, hopeless, lonely, pity party of a mess. Not seeing a way out. Not seeing how anything could get better or how my life mattered anymore. I was desperate. And I was searching for something to get me out of the realm I was living in. Like, I didn't need to change one or two things. I needed a whole new life. And I didn't see how that could be possible. So, in my human mind, with overwhelming despair trapped in my emotions, the only thing I could think of was death…

Until I looked on the floorboard of my car and saw that tape again. It must have been one of the drug dealers that left that tape in there (I had CD's too but I decided to keep the tape deck in the '92 Bubble

Chevy — I'm not that old!) On the side of it was written *Divine Revelation of Hell.* Oh yea, *that's* why I never picked up that thing before! Are you kidding? I had never heard the word revelation, but I had sure heard the word hell. I knew nothing about it, but it didn't sound pleasant. I think it sat on the floorboard for two weeks. But on that day in April, I was desperate and willing to try anything. So, I reached down and picked it up, stuck it in the player, and began to listen.

This lady described different places in hell. For some reason, God had literally taken her to hell, in the spirit, to these actual places in hell. As she was talking, it was like I was right there with her. (I was not high at the time). It was so very real…and *terrifying.* The entire place was filled with hot fire. And thousands of prisons cells. I'm not even sure if I want to describe all of it to you. But there were people there. Lots of people. One person to each cell. Tormented. And screaming. I was in a cell, all by myself, pressed up against the back wall trying to get away from these wildly hot scorching flames that were chasing after me. They were reaching out for me, taunting me, trying to burn me up. But it didn't burn me up. I couldn't believe it wasn't burning me up. I kept trying to get away from it but there was no escape. The worst part was the loneliness. The extreme loneliness felt like this Grand Canyon-sized deep void within my gut that could never ever be filled. It was painful. The most painful thing I had ever experienced. I was all alone, being tormented, and there was nothing I could do.

I was terrified.

I knew that was where I was going. In fact, while partying in Daytona Beach at the age of 15 or 16 a few years prior, I overdosed and was dying. Everything was black and dark and I was being sucked up into this scary, black hole and kept saying, "Mom! Don't let them take me now! No! I can't go now! Mom, help me!" I was unconscious, possibly dead, but woke up shortly after I was screaming and begging "them" not to take me. The tape I listened to in my Chevy Caprice explained where I was going on that day and why I was so afraid.

I was almost paralyzed while listening to that tape in my car. But as quick as the terrifying realization of hell came over me, another realization came. God existed. Suddenly, I felt really small. And I could sense *God*, this giant God, right above me. I suddenly knew He existed, but I wasn't afraid of Him. Rather, I was afraid because I *didn't* know Him, and something in me knew that I was *supposed* to know Him. And in another instant, I suddenly believed in Him! And then I got filled with hope! Right after I believed in Him, I was filled with hope, a power that came and set me free.

My addiction was broken! God revealed Himself to me, then set me free from my drug addiction. I looked down at the drugs that were in my car with a new set of air in my lungs, and said out loud, "I don't have to do this anymore!" I rolled down my window, threw them out, regretting it for a moment thinking I should at least sell them, but then came to my senses and kept driving.

I don't remember the phone calls. But I ended up detoxing at a neighbor's house and checked into a rehab shortly after. This was a *new beginning* for me. I met God. He met me in that car. I have no idea why He used those situations to bring me to Him. Hell?! Are you serious? I know, it may seem…. I have no idea how it seems to you. But this is what I can tell you. God is good! He is so good! My sins were sending me straight to that place and God rescued me from it all! I thank God for all the prayers that my friends and family prayed for me. He answered their prayers.

Psalm 107: 10-16

"Some sat in darkness and deepest gloom, imprisoned in iron chains of misery. They rebelled against the words of God, scorning the counsel of the Most High. That is why he broke them with hard labor; they fell, and no one was there to help them. "Lord, Help!" they cried in their trouble, and He saved them from their distress. He led them from the darkest and deepest gloom; he snapped their chains. Let them praise the Lord for His great love and for the wonderful things He has done for them. For He broke down their prison gates of bronze; He cut apart their bars of iron."

# 4

# Talking to God

It was all real. I came to believe in God. I completed the rehab and went back to college. I was hopeful; had no doubt I would succeed. I was clean and sober and started praying a little, but I was young and wanted to play more than work on my sobriety and relationship with God. My wise counselors were "fun" and "folly": the odd notion that somehow passing college classes was an automatic ticket into success and life was a party. Fun and folly turned out to be nothing more than immaturity and a lack of surrender…that turned into a relapse.

Oops.

I'll spare you the details of the amount of darkness and despair I found myself in for those last two years. The shameful things I did brought me to such a low place that I had nothing left…I didn't even feel human. But it was about to be all over. **I had surrendered.** I found out I had warrants in several counties and called the police on myself. I don't know if I actually said this (I cannot quite remember) but I'm pretty sure I said; "I am a danger to society. Y'all need to come and get me! This is my address." Believe it or not, it took them a week to get me! But when they did, the officer let me sit in the front seat and escorted me to my new home.

Jail was a blessing! I was rescued from that awful drug lifestyle and it's the place where I really got to know God. God had placed hope in me as I stood in that jail cell. I *believed* in Him. I *knew* that He existed. He saw me. And He could help me. I felt comforted and was not afraid. And it was all going to be alright.

By day two or three in that jail cell, after some of the drugs wore off and I was a bit more coherent, I clearly remember looking up at God, and thinking, "God, all I want is You. I don't care if I have to do 15 years in prison. I just don't want to go back to that way of life and all I want is You." I was facing 15 years, but I had the most peace I ever had simply because I surrendered and took responsibility for what I had done. And God had put His love in my heart.

By day three or four, I wasn't sleeping. I used to be an insomniac, so when the sleepless nights started rolling in, I put my foot down. No way. I am NOT dealing with this again. Somehow, I knew I needed the bible. Instinctually, I picked it up, went back to my cot, randomly opened it up and it landed on Proverbs 23:4: "Do not be afraid. Thy sleep shall be sweet." I was like whaaaaa?!! No way! Did anyone see this?! That was my first real encounter while reading the bible: it spoke directly to my situation and I believed what I read. I slept like a baby. After that night, I trusted the bible.

I distinctly remember that first week in jail reading the bible. I forgot what I read, but it *knew* me. Like, it knew things about me that I didn't even know! It knew my heart; the innermost parts of my being. It felt so good, so comforting, to be fully known like that.

I think it was the best environment to learn how to pray and read the bible in. There was nothing else to do and everyone was pretty desperate. We were all in very humble positions, not knowing what the outcome of our crimes would be. Some would lose their children. Some would go to prison for years, others just received a slap on the wrist. But there was a sense of desperation which broke us just enough to let God in and surrender our way of doing things.

For six months I read the bible and talked to God daily, especially at night or in the morning while I was lying in bed (if you can call that one-inch old mat on concrete a bed). Talking to God was comforting and even fun. Sometimes I felt a little crazy. I told Him *everything*. Imagine hosting a sleepover at your house for your 9-year-old daughter and her girlfriends. They would chatter all night if you would let them. How can they even talk that much?! LOL. I talked to God like that. I told him all about my day and verbalized every single thought in my head and feeling that was in my heart. I would often get answers back, gain clarity, and would always feel relieved (Psalm 51:6). But I didn't *always* believe God was there, which is why I wondered if I was crazy sometimes. It takes faith to believe in something that is invisible, ya know?

I became good friends with my bunkie who, one day, asked me if I wanted to pray with her. "Like, *out loud?*" I asked. "Um, yes," she said sarcastically, as if like, "Duh!" I don't remember ever seeing people pray together…like ever. (I wasn't raised in church as a kid and had no clue about church people). Anyway, so my bunkie told me to hold her hands and just pray out loud. So, I did. Very robotic- like. "Dear Jesus….". It was awkward and sounded nothing like it did when I talked to God on my bed at night. I never started my prayers off with "Dear Jesus", I just started talking because I knew He was already there. But, I did it. That was my first experience praying with another person and I'll never forget it.

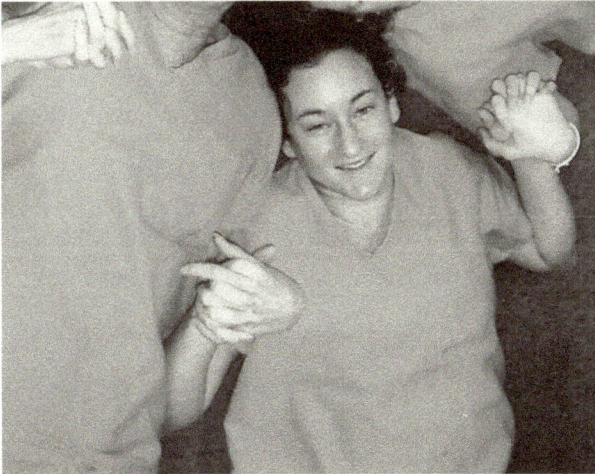

Me on the floor with the other inmates in jail. Instead of 15 years, I served 6 months in jail and 1 year in rehab.

# 5

## BORN AGAIN

I had such a drastic change from the dark sinful world I was living in to a life with Jesus. I had this intense desire to be clean and holy (mostly because I had felt so dirty from all the shameful things I had done). I was also very sensitive to angels and demons that were flying about in the air and in people's lives. I reacted to the world around me like I just got electrocuted. I didn't know how to deal with what I was sensing and was *shocked* at the level of immorality in our nation and was in a bit of a panic to eradicate it all (especially the sin that was still in my own life). I saw how present God was in our midst and how much He loves us, but most how people were completely unaware of His existence at all! Probably the thing that hurt/frustrated me the most was the condition of the church. I fell in love with Jesus and some of the churches I went to…I mean, the people looked dead. Lifeless. Expressionless. I was in a state of shock. Do they even *know* the same Jesus I know?!

It was like I suddenly woke up. And I wanted to wake everyone else up as well. I think that was part of my *born-again* experience. I didn't read any book besides the bible for a while. My thinking was so jacked up and I didn't trust people very much. But I knew I could trust the truth that is in the Word. I didn't care who said what, I was going to God on it! Holy Spirit is my Teacher, not man.

When I believed in, and surrender my life to Jesus, He gave me His Holy Spirit and took away my sin nature. He gave me *His* nature. And another shift came after an "Encounter" weekend at this new church I found. I got baptized in the Holy Spirit and woke up the next morning feeling like a completely different person. I was born again. Not from my mother's womb, but from heaven. My body never changed, but death left my soul and life came in…eternal life. Bought and paid for by Jesus. It was like some crazy alien encounter. I mean, I didn't ride in a spaceship. But if you think about it, the reason I was suddenly in a state of shock at the world around me was because I was no longer born "from this world." I was from another world, a heavenly place, and I got sent down from heaven and was now living on this fallen planet. My spiritual sight was opened up and I saw the world with a new perspective. I was a new creation. (John 6:38, 1 Peter 1:23, John 3:3, 1 Corinthians 2:12, John 15:19, John 8:23, Ephesians 1:21).

## Prophecy, Healing, Miracles

Everywhere I went, I looked around and wondered if that person knew God. How are they doing? They are limping, it looks like they need prayer for healing. And, so I did. I went up to people all the time, anywhere and anytime, and asked if they wanted prayer. I believed what the bible said and that Jesus told us to pray for these things and I had the power of the Holy Spirit upon me, giving me a grace and boldness to walk this out. As I was daily discovering how much God loved me, it spilled out of me. I was young and immature in the faith, but it didn't matter. I was the woman at the well who met Jesus and wanted to tell everyone about Him. It seemed kind of natural.

I also remember a time when I did not enjoy being around people. LOL. I was *so uncomfortable* around them! I had anxiety and would leave hangouts wondering what they thought of me or would rehearse all the things I said or thought "wrong." And sometimes, I just didn't like people; for no reason. I prayed a very specific prayer for years because the hypocrisy really bothered me. "God, help me to love people! Help me to see them the way that *You* see them!"

I found that the more I ran to Him for my own freedom (from anxiety, stress, fear, shame, torment, etc.), the more love I had for others. I found tools (prophecy, healing, love, the Word) and a burden to help them with their own bondages. Psalm 118 says it perfectly and depicted my first decade with the Lord. I'd cry out to Him for deliverance, He'd part the clouds and come down to rescue me, show me how much He loved me, and then train my hands for battle to help others get set free too. I took what happened in the place of prayer and bible study into my church, work, grocery stores, places I'd volunteer...anywhere there were people.

I even got to preach in the same jail...*the same cell pod*...that I was locked up in years prior! God rarely gave me a prepared messaged. I would ask, but He just had me show up. I was always nervous. *God, are you going to show up today? I feel irresponsible not being well prepared.* But He always told me that the time I spent in prayer *was* preparation. I'd walk in, introduce myself and then close my eyes and wait on the Holy Spirit. He came every time! Holy Spirit would move powerfully for the women in that jail! For three years I did this. It was awesome to flow in that kind of anointing.

## Father's Heart

Ahhhh, those early years of my faith were awesome! But I wouldn't go back. I was unstable in my emotions. LOL. And I was quite the orphan.

Ten years ago, when I was going through those early frustrations with the church, the Lord spoke to me and told me not to shake the baby. He said it was "shaken baby syndrome" and the body of Christ was in an infancy stage. In my immaturity, impatience, ignorance, and frustrations, I was angrily shaking the body of Christ in a way that would not have brought life, but death. God *does* say that the violent take the kingdom by force (Matthew 11:12), and yes, I was storming the gates of hell in intercession on behalf of the body of Christ, but I was sometimes misdirected in that zeal and found myself angry at the people. I was absolutely right in what I saw, but I went about it all the wrong way. I didn't quite have the "Father's heart" in my approach and lacked the compassion, patience, wisdom, and gentleness that our heavenly Father has when He addresses issues in the family. I heard the accusing whispers of the enemy, most of it was true and easy to side with. satan was right in many situations, but his accusations came with judgment, condemnation, and panic; get it straight "or else." My Father is infinite in mercy. He does directly confront sin, but with a heart that seeks restoration in the relationship. It's all about the attitude behind it that tells us if correction is coming from our Father or the enemy. (But be careful, not many of us like to be corrected. We may *feel* condemned simply because that is how we are used to responding to correction. Learn to see His correction this way: Hebrews 12:4-13.)

We, as the body of Christ, are NO LONGER in an infancy stage, but we still must be gentle in our dealings with one another and not let our own frustrations cause us to violently shake one another. Passion that comes from the Spirit of God is good, but make sure that passion does not from an offended or self-righteous heart. Jesus said many would be offended because of Him and His ways, but let us not be the ones causing offense because of our own stupidity or immaturity (speaking to myself here).

**Serving**

A few years down the road, I entered into a new season, a focused time of running a business and getting to know a man God brought into my life. I can't say for sure that *God* had me put the miracles on the backburner while I developed character, but that's what ended up happening. It was a really tough season and I was very afraid that I had lost my mojo. I had moved to a new state and, while I was much closer to my blood family, I had lost my church family. I almost completely stopped praying for people. I walked by people and didn't even care to offer prayer, which freaked me out because this just wasn't me. I was confused, frustrated, and afraid. Man, it was tough!

I had a sense that God was maturing me and showing me how to love in a much deeper way, but everything was so muddled up that I wasn't exactly sure. I was afraid of being deceived and didn't trust Him, so I cried out, "God, how can serving *one man* be more important than seeing one million souls saved?! And what am I doing with this business?!" I wanted to make absolutely sure that if God was telling me to lay my vision down, that it was truly Him and not me walking away from Him. I had big vision and promises that I was believing for, but God had me set that on the shelf in order to pursue this man's vision instead of running after my own.

It *felt* like I had let all of my dreams go and that they would never come back. It *felt* like I had just settled for slavery to *someone else's* dreams. But that's not at all what the kingdom of God is like! Jesus says that it is ONLY when you give up your life do you actually find it! This is why is it important to rely on what the Word says and not your emotions. ;)

It was more important to God that I learn to love and respect my husband, than pray for a million souls to come into the kingdom and neglect my husband. There is divine order in the kingdom of God and when things are out of order, it leads to chaos. God was also restoring me to my femininity and teaching me about how He created men to be in their masculinity and how to team up with one. As you can imagine, after having read about my past, I had many soul ties to break and more healing and deliverance than you can imagine. I was clueless about relationships but He was faithful to give me godly examples in the church and restore me, piece by piece.

Anyway, I found that the anointing was not only found in the place of prophecy, healing, and miracles, but in *serving*. God began to reveal the nature of Jesus by giving me a deep desire to serve my husband and the people in my business. And, He was teaching me not to idolize the gifts, miracles, or power. Keep love the main thing.

## Love and Power

It's easy to operate in giftings that are freely given to us by Holy Spirit. It's not as easy to learn to love. And at the end of the day, it's all about love. Jesus said to those who came to Him with a list of all the miracles they "did for Him", "Depart from Me, I never knew you." They had not developed their relationship with Jesus. They had not prioritized love. At the same time, we are warned not to associate with believers who "have a form of godliness but deny its power" (2 Timothy 3:5). We need both character and supernatural movement of the Spirit in power, but to keep love the main thing.

The anointing is not only in miracles; it is in every place that He has called us to walk in. In fact, there are many "grace gifts" found in Romans 12:6-8. I once met a man who ministered deliverance to people all over the world for eight years and then it was like God turned off that gift and directed him into another area of service. So, it doesn't matter, so long as we are joyfully obeying the Lord and spending time with Him to find out what He is wanting to do in and through our lives.

Being born again starts with your personal belief in Jesus Christ and a baptism of His Spirit, bringing you into the family of God, making you whole, and giving you power to make a difference in the world around you. Being born again is a wonderful experience, but the fullness happens in community. I guarantee you it will be challenging to be in close relationship with others, but the reward is so great! It is worth it to face your own issues and to help others face theirs…with the goal of sincere devotion to God and selfless love toward one another. I love you. I am so grateful for the many people God has placed in my life. I wouldn't be here today without them. I hope you not only place your faith in Jesus Christ and ask for a baptism of the Holy Spirit, but you seek out community with those who call on the Lord with a sincere heart (2 Timothy 2:22).

# 6

## Israel, Part One

One day my client called me on the phone and asked me if I wanted to go with her to Israel, that I would pay my own way, but her husband didn't want to go and she felt led to ask me. The moment she asked me I could feel the Holy Spirit hit my tummy and I started laughing. I didn't understand it, but immediately sensed that God was up to something and said, "Well, I guess I'm going to Israel!"

When I landed in Tel Aviv for the first time and stepped out of the plane, I felt like I was home. I cannot quite recall ever feeling that way, even my own hometown…*and my mom still lives in the house I grew up in*! But yea, Israel felt like a different kind of home.

I went with one of my clients and her two friends. We had no tour guide. We knew nothing. We even lost our map. We would step outside of our hostel and just start walking, asking Holy Spirit to lead us. I was so grateful for Holy Spirit. We had His indwelling presence inside us, guiding us, showing us the way to go. Everyone else seemed to have an outward devotion, but did they have His Spirit living inside them? It was sad. An outward devotion is like being blindfolded and having to feel your way through the dark. You cannot see where to go! But when Jesus sent us His very Spirit to live inside of us, it's like we can see! We may not know *everything*, but we can know *Him* and can hear His faint whispers to teach us and lead us. We saw many things as we walked all over Jerusalem. It was incredible.

The second or third night there, I was lying in bed and just about had a faith crisis. I saw Muslims and Jews, wholeheartedly devoted to their faith. I barely saw that in America. But here, they are…*devoted*! And I thought to myself, *is Jesus even real?! How do I know Jesus is real?!* It freaked me out to question my faith like that. But instead of trying to figure it out on my own, I brought those questions to the Lord and He immediately spoke to my heart, "It's by faith you believe." That's it. It's by faith. There is no "proof" other than what is revealed to me through the scriptures and what I've experienced. Taking my logical mind out of the equation, I responded back to the Lord with my heart, "Yes I believe that Jesus is real and He is God."

Our hostel was right above a small grocery store. I went to buy something one day and as I was paying at the cash register, this man beside me asked me to pray for him. I slowly turned my head to see who this man was: a Muslim man, much taller than me. I was nervous but he was so desperate looking and I said okay. I paid for my things and told him I'd meet him outside. When we got on the sidewalk, he began to tell me that his whole family follows Islam, but he follows

Jesus. He grew up devoted to Allah, but had cancer that was spread all in his body and had a dream about Jesus one night and Jesus healed him. He began following Jesus after that, but his family didn't know. If they knew, they would kill him. And he asked me to pray for him simply because he was lonely in his faith and somehow knew I was a believer. I was inspired by his story and prayed with him.

Just as we were finishing praying, the store clerk came out and stood right beside him, arms crossed, and very seriously looked at me. I thought for sure he was going to try to kill me. But instead I asked, "Can I help you?" He said, "Yes, tell me about this Jesus." I was taken back in amazement, but still thought he was trying to trick me in order to hurt me or kill me, but I felt it was okay and started talking.

God is so good. Even when we stumble through, trying to find the words to say, He shows up and helps us. The first question I asked was *brilliant* (high five, God!): "You pray right?" He looked at me and didn't say anything. I said, "You pray to Allah, right?" And he said, "Of course, of course." "Good," I said. "Does he talk back to you when you pray?" He reacted, slightly offended, "No, no." With joy I said, "Jesus talks back!" He looked at me like I was crazy. To them, it's almost blasphemy to even consider for Allah to talk with humans. Their god is holy and does not get on the level to talk with humans: there is no relationship there. The only way they can go to paradise (heaven) is to live a good life, follow the Koran, and *hope* they are accepted (kind of like how many Americans are). Anyway, it was a nice conversation and because he was still curious, I asked if it was okay if I came back at another time to talk with him again.

So, I did. At midnight. By myself. My friend felt a peace about letting me go alone and stayed up to pray for me. When I got there, he got straight to the point and asked a rather intrusive question: "Have you ever had sex?" I was about to run when he said that. I thought for sure I had completely mistaken his curiosity for the gospel. But, I asked him what he meant, and he asked me the same thing again. I told him I was not going to tell him my personal information. So, he rephrased it: "It is not lawful for us to have sex outside of marriage. I have had sex and am not married. Can I be forgiven? Does your God forgive of this sin?"

His pure, childlike desire to be cleansed and forgiven astounded me. (It's a rare and beautiful thing to meet someone who is eager to be forgiven). I said, "Yes, of course! Just ask Him to!" He asked, "How do I stand when I pray and ask to be forgiven? Like this?" (He folded his hands together as if to pray). I was a little confused because it doesn't matter how we fold our hands or how we pray. I figured his culture or religion had taught him maybe some way to pray or stand as a form of respect, which is awesome, but it has nothing to do with salvation. I told him, "Oh no, no. It doesn't matter how we stand. What matters is what *Jesus* did. He is God. He died for our sins. When you believe this, you ask Him to forgive you, and He does!"

This was a foreign concept to him. He asked me many questions that night and had so many thoughts swirling around through his mind. He asked me what I was doing that I was up so late (it was midnight, remember?) I said, well, there was a bombing in the American Embassy in Lebanon and I was afraid. But God told me to go dance on the roof of our hostel. So, I did. It broke the fear right off of me as I danced and got filled with joy. I was so full of energy (His Spirit), that I asked him what I could do next. He told me to come down and talk to you. So, I did. ☺

JERUSALEM – THE WESTERN WALL

# 7

# THE ULTIMATE MERCY

I drove about four hours near Miami to visit my friend who was serving a 15-year sentence. As always when visiting an inmate in prison, you have to wait. I got through security but had to wait at least an hour in the visitation room while they pulled her out. In the meantime, I started talking to another inmate (which you're not supposed to do…but I have a big mouth and couldn't help myself☺.) We were pretty discrete. She was really kind. About my age. Nice conversation.

Then my friend finally came out and found me sitting at the table. We slid down the bench a bit for more privacy, and she looked at me and said, "Why were you talking to her?" I'm like, uh, you know me, right? LOL. My friend's crime was a felony robbery charge, but no one got hurt and it was a ridiculous sentence. But most of the women in her cell block were in for murder, and that particular woman I was talking to had killed her *mother*.

I couldn't believe it. *Her?* That sweet, *normal* girl? Her own *mom?!* What happened?! How could she do that? Her own mother! I had so many questions, but since our visit was short, we focused the conversation on catching up.

I felt like I was walking in slow motion as I walked out of the prison parking lot that day. It was so good to see my friend, but very sobering. First of all, that should have been me in that prison. I was the one who was supposed to serve 15. I counted it up. I would have had eight years left had I been sentenced that day. But instead, I got the rehab and she relapsed and ended up with the 15.

And secondly, that other *girl!* The girl who killed her mother. I was still in shock. As soon as I got in my car, I began to weep. I mean, tears started flowing down my cheeks like a flood. I was sobbing in grief. I couldn't believe it. I sat there for a moment, a little stunned at how deeply that had affected me. And then I pulled it together enough to feel safe to actually start driving.

But waves of grief kept hitting me. I gripped the steering wheel. It was as if it was me. It was as if I had killed my mother. I was put in her shoes for a moment. I felt the worst sense of dread imaginable. **Dread.** What have I done? I can't take it back. I can't take it back. She's dead. And there is nothing I can do about it. I can't take it back!

And then I remembered *Jesus.* Jesus, how can you forgive her? It doesn't make any sense. How can a good God forgive someone who killed their own mother? I began to seriously doubt His goodness. I couldn't wrap my mind around it. It didn't make any sense. Like zero. What-so-ever. It made no sense. How can you forgive that?

And then I started talking to myself. Okay, Ashleigh. This is the gospel

that you are preaching. Do you believe, like truly believe, in the very gospel that you are preaching? At that moment, my faith was challenged.

Even though it still made no sense, I believed the bible. And I said, yes. Jesus, I don't get it, but I believe that you died, you paid a high price to forgive people of their sins...even the sin of murder...even murdering one's own mother. My feelings didn't agree with it, but my faith did. My feelings were pretty conflicted, but I did believe that if she asked Jesus to forgive her, that she would be forgiven.

(I won't even begin to try and explain how God's mercy came through for her mom, but I know God is good. I don't have the answers to that or why she had to die. The only perspective I have is how the girl can be forgiven if she asks Jesus to forgive her, of even the most heinous crime, because Jesus took her sins for her.)

God does not hold that against her, or even treat her like a murderer. She is a restored daughter. That's the part that blows me away. You still love her, welcome her into your arms, and hold nothing against her?! But yea. That's the gospel. As far as the east is from the west, so He removes our sins from us.

It wasn't *just* for Jesus to die. He was sinless and didn't deserve to die. That was the biggest injustice ever done. An innocent man died yet, unlike some of us, He was not at fault or a victim. He willingly obeyed the Father's perfect will which was to be mistreated and abused, even to the point of death, on our behalf. He is now sitting at the right hand of the Father and will rule and reign as King forever. His reward is very great.

It matters how you deal with the injustice you see in your life. Our Father will reward you for obeying Him in how you handle each situation of injustice. One thing I do know is that forgiveness is a must. See His naked body nailed to that cross and worship Him for the price He paid to forgive you. Everlasting mercy has been given to you.

When injustice is happening, I tend to see this aspect of God, even for the criminal, the perpetrator, the guilty party. It does not excuse their behavior, rather, I cry out to God for mercy on their behalf. Like Jesus said about those who were nailing Him to the cross, "Forgive them, for they do not know what they are doing."

Knowing God's mercy doesn't mean that we don't stand up and take action against the injustice we see. Oh no, there is definitely a time to stand up, speak up, take action, and bring a solution for the problems that sin causes. It's just that, we need to see God's mercy as well so that we don't cause more problems. We truly need God's wisdom and His ways in all circumstances.

# 8

# EXPERIENCES IN PRAYER

I want to share three experiences that impacted my prayer life and relationship with God: Worshippers, My Room, and Stopping a War.

**Worshippers**

I told you before that some of my experiences in church were religious and with people who seemed to lack love and passion for Jesus. But it wasn't long before I found a Spirit filled environment. I was so hungry for the things of God that I found myself at another church's youth service on Wednesday nights. Mind you, I was 25 at the time, not exactly the same age as all the other 15 and 16-year olds who attended. But I didn't care. Worship was amazing. And I needed some major healing from my crazy past, as well as, connect with other believers who were moving in the things of the Spirit.

It wasn't just the five songs everyone knew which ended abruptly so the preaching could start. It was <u>prophetic worship</u> where we lingered in the presence of God and had time to commune with His Spirit. During this worship, I would find myself on the floor crying, crawled up in one of the girl's laps who just held me, or dancing freely, shouting with exuberance, praying with authority, and worshipping Jesus with my whole heart, mind, soul, and strength.

We are worshipping a real God, not a distant or imaginary "hope He exists" kind of a God. We need TIME to linger there for a while so we can get answers to our problems and encounter Him. Worship is not about singing songs. It's about allowing Him to reveal Himself to us and connecting with Him. It's not about performance or what this person or that person does. It was about His PRESENCE and getting to know Jesus Christ. It was about His presence coming into our sanctuary and overflowing into the rest of our lives and into our city.

That is what I found in that little church of worshippers. I found a place where I could be myself, a place where the anointing was strong enough to break chains off of me and set me free, a place that helped me to connect to God and pray faith-filled, powerful prayers for other people and *with* other people. Ask Him to release a spirit of grace and supplication upon you (Zechariah 12:10) so that you can pray more effectively.

Wherever I go in the world, I look for a house of prayer where I can worship with other believers.

## My Room

I cannot remember the timing of this one, but it was around the same time I was learning about worship and "spending time" with God. I moved in with two wonderful new roomies. Almost immediately, God spoke to me and said, "Spend time with Me." I didn't know what He meant, and like many times when God speaks, I'm not always 100% sure that was even Him. But I continued the conversation with Him with an *attitude* (I used to have such an attitude with Him and would question everything. LOL). I said, "And do *what?*" He replied, "Just spend time with me in your room." I'm like, "Yea fine but what do you want me to do?" Anyway, I felt like He said to choose two nights a week and just go to my room and we would figure it out. So, I did.

Those two nights a week were AMAZING. No matter what my roommates were doing or what was going on, I had an incredible grace to discipline myself to those nights. Believing what He says always comes with a power to walk it out. Belief is so powerful, especially when that belief takes root.

Those two nights a week lasted over two years, which turned into another two years, and continue to this day. I would often turn my laptop on to that house of prayer that was being live streamed. There was an outpouring happening during that year and all of these people were getting healed. As I listened to their testimonies, I would get set free too, because hope came in. I believed it could happen for me too. And it did. A ton of emotional healing.

I'd also sit in silence and just wait on Him to come and meet with me or direct our time together. The bible would direct me, convict me, strengthen me, or give me insight into a situation. It wasn't always magical, but I don't think I ever left that place unchanged. I also began to pray with deep groanings (Romans 8:26) for the clients at the rehab and jail I was teaching at. God was giving me His heart and anointed me to love them and set them free. So, in the previous chapters when I mentioned that I would pray for people and I saw hundreds get healed, this is where the anointing came.

The gifts and anointing of God are free. You don't work for it. But He did say to "Tarry in the city (in my room) until you are clothed with power from on high." *The more I spent time with Him (without an agenda) the more anointed I got.*

### Stopping a War

An intifada (a war) was on the horizon. Every day for at least a week an awful terrorist attack was occurring in Jerusalem. It wasn't in mass numbers, but it was horrific and increasing daily. Someone ran into a synagogue and stabbed several people just a few blocks from where I was living. Another day someone ran their car off the road and hit a pedestrian. It went on and on every day for over a week. When you're in Israel and stuff like that starts happening, it's not an isolated event. The entire nation is under attack and it feels like the whole world wants to bomb you.

About that time, I got really sick. I ended up in my room, for three days straight, unable to go out or even hear what was going on. It was a good thing: God didn't want me to watch the news and panic. He wanted me to be in the Word and see what He was doing. And

He wanted me in peace. So, I trusted Him and laid low.

When I started feeling better, the house of prayer director called a meeting to deal with what was happening and we met in the prayer house. I'll never forget this. We all got in the Spirit, focusing on Jesus, and a worship leader led us into some songs. We praised the name of the Lord and as we exalted Him above the city, prophetic words and visions began to come.

A man saw this large demon hovering over Jerusalem. And it was inciting violent attacks in the city. It would put thoughts in people's minds and the people would carry out the attacks. But then, he saw a larger angel lock up the demon in this type of prison with a sign over it that said "not now." As he described what he was seeing, we all came into agreement that the time for these violent attacks was "not now" and we settled into a time of rest and peace.

Right after that, all the violence came to a halt. Not one incident happened after that, not for a period of time anyway. You could literally feel the hush, the tangible peace, come back into the city again. And I was amazed.

How can God stop a war through our prayers?! Or was it that He was just waiting for His people to pray and come into agreement with what He was already doing or wanting to do? I do not know the semantics of what happened, but I do know that prayer and worship is powerful. It's a place to defeat the enemy.

FYI, the greatest spiritual battle in the world is over that piece of land. satan wants to be god and has made some bold statements in Isaiah 14 about setting his throne *above* Yahweh's throne. It was the very reason he got kicked out of heaven: pride. He wanted to be god. And still does. So, he fights, especially over Jerusalem, but he will never win. When Jesus returns, He will lock satan up, set up His throne as King of kings on Mount Zion in Jerusalem, and rule forever (Zechariah 14:16-17).

I could often feel the intensity of that spiritual battle, but would sense God *laughing* at the plans of the enemy (Psalm 2). No matter how much the enemy rages, God remains 100% peaceful, with no worries, secure in His position as God. So much so, that He actually laughs at the fact that satan even tries. I visualized this in my mind as I'd look out onto the Mount and would laugh too. I wasn't provoking satan or mocking disrespectfully like how he mocks. Rather, the laughter came from a place of victory from the Lord. That's why, even in the midst of violent attacks, we can remain peaceful and victorious…because our God is King.

# 9

# *ISRAEL, PART TWO*

Okay, so after the first time I went to Israel, something inside of me was definitely stirred for that nation, but I had little understanding of it.

This whole Israel thing was *not* my idea. When I was a personal trainer and working on a bachelor's degree in psychology, I had vision for prison ministry, utilizing my knowledge and skills to bring wholeness to the inmates. I had *plans* for this and even gathered ten board members for the non-profit that I would be starting.

The day we were supposed to meet, not one person could come! I was so bummed, but before I could get discouraged, I went into prayer and this messianic worship music came on. I was on my knees when the Lord spoke and said, "I have not called you out of your job for prison ministry, I have called you out to pray for Israel." I looked up at Him like He was crazy. "Um…Lord, how am I supposed to make a living *praying for Israel?* Like what does that even mean?" But I had this sense that if I said yes, I would be taken care of and I would be so blessed. So, I said yes…and the blessings down.

I asked Him where to start, and He said something to the effect of, "Just start reading the bible where it talks about Israel. Don't start reading books and listening to other people's opinions yet." I had this sense that people can have some odd ideas that are not biblical concerning Israel and God wanted to teach me straight from His Word until I got a solid foundation. I read quite a bit in Genesis chapters 12-17, Ephesians, Zechariah, Romans 9-11, Jeremiah and Isaiah. After spending a year or so reading the bible about Israel, and interceding out of Isaiah 49 with a small worship team, I learned quite a bit, but I couldn't quite grasp it all.

I didn't know what to do with the whole Israel thing. It still seemed to have nothing to do with *my* life, so I lost interest for a while. God encouraged me to start praying for Israel again and get back on board, but I didn't really listen. After some time went by, He woke me up out of a dream one night. Actually, it was more like a severe warning of some kind: "If you don't pray for Israel, I'll find someone else who will." Yikes! Okay, okay. At that moment, I suddenly realized what a privilege it was to be chosen to pray for Israel and that it was more special to Him than I ever understood. I had a feeling that I could do prison ministry and my life would still be "good" but not the "best" that He had for me.

I believe that our Christian faith is not just about us having a better life. It's about us participating in what God is doing on the earth, partnering with His Word, being an active family member in the work that God is doing on the earth, ultimately, because we love God

and want to be as close to Him as possible. *That* is why this Israel stuff is important to me. It's because I love God that I care about what He cares about. To be disinterested in His Word or not even ask what is on HIS heart is an easy trap to fall into, but it's not a trap we want to stay in. To be married to someone and only think of *your* interests makes for an unhappy marriage.

Anyway, God ordered my steps, one by one, and I found myself living in Israel for 3 months. It was miraculous: I raised $10,000 in 2 weeks for that trip. The people of God gave generously: they wanted to bless Israel but couldn't go themselves.

We lived in Jerusalem but traveled all throughout Izzy (I sometimes call Israel that). We prayed for Israel and the nations. I felt an authority in prayer. Isaiah 2:3 says, "for the Word of the Lord will go out from Zion." We were taught by some of the best teachers in the world. They emphasized the "one new man" in which Jew and Gentile would come together in Messiah (Ephesians 2:15). Then and only then will there be peace in Israel. They unraveled Isaiah 19, which my spirit immediately grabbed ahold of. And I began to realize that in my personal study times the year before, I had learned quite a bit: I wasn't as lost as I thought.

I made life-long friends during that time and heard God tell me that I would go back and forth there for the rest of my life. A desire to bring others there grew. It was more than a mission trip. It is a calling.

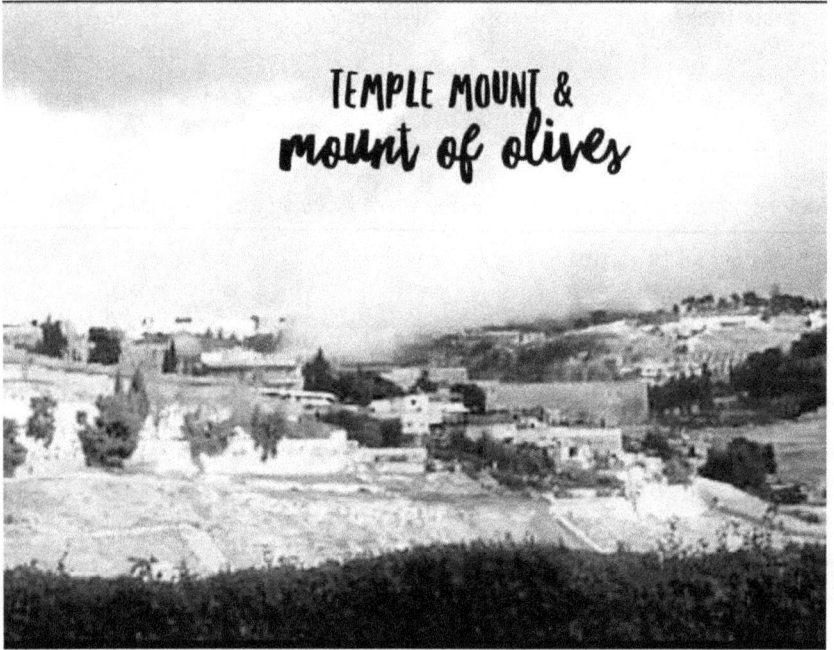

TEMPLE MOUNT &
*mount of olives*

# 10

# SELL IT ALL AND GO!

During my last month living in Israel in 2014, I began to ask the Lord what His plans were for me when I got back into the states. In prayer one day, I felt like the He told me to "sell all of my belongings and follow Him." I was getting a real burden for America and got the sense that He wanted to send me throughout America, praying for people and praying for the nation. But I didn't have a clue on how I was going to support myself, where I would go, or how that would work out. I needed some scripture to back up what I was hearing because it sounded completely crazy. He gave me Luke 9.

Being single for so long gave me the opportunity to rely on the Lord in emotional and practical ways. I fell asleep talking to Him, I woke up with Him, and spent most of my free time reading the Word, listening to sermons, attending church services, worshipping and praying. I became accustomed to seeking His will in every area of my life. I allowed His Word to govern my heart and guide my footsteps.

I have about 30 journals from where I would pour my thoughts out and God would prophetically speak to me. He was my best friend

and I did my best to live by every word that proceeded out of His mouth. So, when He asked me to "sell everything and follow Him", it was a stretch, but not a far stretch. I just did what I was already doing: I spent time with Him and He told me what to do next or opened a door.

One week after I got back from Israel, I sold what furniture and belongings I had remaining, adopted my beloved cat out, and hit the road. For almost two years, I traveled like a homeless bum...LOL. Sorry, I wasn't a homeless bum, but it sure did feel like it at times! Anyway, it was a very adventurous year. I was blessed by the hospitality of people I knew and didn't know. The way that God chose to lead me forced me to rely on Him...and other people for my most basic needs. I was humiliated slash humbled. I accepted the invitations to stay with people, knowing that God would bless them for hosting me. I got to live with people and get to know them for who they really are...not just for the masks they wear out in the world. And I even met my husband during that time!

In spite of this courage, confidence, faith, whatever you want to call it, I was also afraid...especially about provision, and would often slip into deep feelings of shame because I wasn't earning my own money anymore. I *had* no money. I didn't know where it was going to come from. I didn't want *anyone* to know it, and yet I wanted *everyone* to know it, recognize the good work I was doing for God, and eagerly send me money so I could do my job and not worry about provision (which is why I have a heart to support missionaries). I was also very lonely at times and longed to be on some sort of team. I couldn't figure out why I was doing all of this "alone" but then again, if I was on a team, I may not have met the people I met. And I may not have seen what God was doing beyond my own denomination. I want to share a few stories of the adventures God took me on while I traveled throughout California over a 3-month period.

## On my way to… Central Cali

One of my favorite times was the California Adventure, attending the School of Prophets with my pastor. LOL. Oh gosh. That was a huge blessing for two reasons. One, the prophetic gift got restored in me. Previously, I was a Jeremiah, Isaiah, an Ezekiel, sent to rebuke everyone out of their sin and apathy and into wholehearted devotion to Jesus. I was feeling the call of a prophet's lifestyle and was deeply convicted, but wasn't walking in mature love. God kept my mouth shut most of the time (and so did the fear of man), but I ultimately knew that I needed the Father's perspective.

1 Corinthians 14:3 says that the gift of prophecy is to strengthen, encourage, and comfort people. I didn't think of my prophetic gift that way until then. I saw it as a tool to discern what was wrong and then bring correction to the body. Which, a prophetic gift *can* be used to bring correction, but with a goal to strengthen, encourage, or comfort…not to punish, accuse, or bring condemnation.

The second reason that School of Prophets was such a blessing: my pastor's wife, my dear friend, felt that it would be really good if her husband and I learned how to work as a team and even sensed that God would restore some things for the both of us. With the former issues I had with men and anyone in authority, combined with my lack of understanding about his giftings, I'd say we clashed from time to time. LOL. While he had own stuff to work out, God gave him a lot of grace and love for me. So, when we went out to the ministry training in Cali and got to actually talk through things and understand each other's hearts, God restored trust and we let go of offense. That was a very special time for me.

## On my way to...Redding then LA

I was so blessed to see my friend in Redding! She wrote a sweet note for me and gave me a book to read. Her new hubby was so fun and took me to work out at a gym. We all just had great fellowship and enjoyed each other; so much grace and love. I stayed about a week, with only one clue on where I was going next.

A few months before I flew out to Cali, I was praying one morning and had a picture in my mind of me on a bus, on my birthday, traveling from Redding to LA. But I doubted it once I got to Redding because I had nowhere to stay in LA and God remained silent every time I'd ask him to confirm what I was supposed to do. The only thing I could rely on was that faint memory of the vision of me on a bus. I decided to stick with that until He told me something else. And so, I waited for Him to reassure me or confirm it. But when that visit was about to be over...*nothing*. I still didn't have any concrete guidance from God. He didn't even speak "take the bus." I just had to rely on what I thought He told me to do months prior. So, by faith, I purchased a bus ticket on my birthday, and headed out to LA, with no plans on what I'd do when I got there.

That 12-hour bus ride was adventurous and nerve racking all at the same time. I kept thinking, "Surely God will connect me with someone in LA who will be waiting for me when I get there, with arms open wide. I'll be welcomed into the city and given a nice place to sleep." I only had $45 in my account, so hotels weren't really an option.

I emailed and messaged some friends, asking for connections, but also didn't want to sound desperate and needy, and I *did* want to rely on God and not make my own way. In the meantime, I decided to read that book that my friend gave me called "Face to Face with Jesus." It was about a Muslim girl in the Middle East who met Jesus. She had a radical encounter with Him and believed that He is God and the Son of God. He brought so much love and life into her heart that she began to tell many people about Him, and was severely persecuted because of it. Story after story of her being beaten or almost raped, mocked, and finally, her church was bombed and she died and came back to life. I was so inspired by her courage to preach the gospel. Her own life didn't matter. She needed to tell others about this God she had found.

I began to think differently about my situation. Like, "Whoa, Ashleigh! Snap out of it! God is sending you to pray for people. *Who cares* where you are going to sleep. Who cares about comforts! All that matters are people knowing their Savior." I resolved to stay at the LA county bus station if I had to. Shortly after, I was praying and had a vision of a nice blanket on the bus station floor with a beautiful rose on it. God was reminding me of my identity as a royal daughter. He wanted to give me dignity before I walked into that bus station.

## LA Bus Station

It was almost midnight when we arrived. I got my suitcase and proceeded into the terminal. I still hoped that someone would appear and take me to their home, but no one, so I found a place to sit down. The family beside me were all crying. They didn't speak much English, but I attempted to ask what was wrong. A family member had died and they were traveling to the funeral. It was a sad situation. A few young kids were with them, and they looked lost, afraid. I don't remember if I prayed for them out loud, but I did in my heart. I got up a few minutes later and walked over to another area. I had a few casual conversations. One man struggled with suicidal thoughts. I prayed for him and wanted something powerful to happen, but we just kept talking. A few hours went by and I realized I had nowhere to go. I laid my head down on my suitcase and slept for a while.

When I woke up, I talked to a few more people and sat there, waiting. Suddenly, this young man came running up to me almost hysterically and said, "I'm addicted to heroin. Please pray for me. I have to get off this stuff." He came out of nowhere and I wasn't praying for anyone else at the time, so I have no idea how he knew to come up to me, but he did. Instead of eagerly praying for him, I asked him if he wanted breakfast. I was hungry and figured he may be too. Breakfast gave me time to talk to him and find out where he was at and how I could pray for him. I think the conversation alone (just being normal) was good for him, and then I prayed for his addiction to be broken in Jesus name.

## On my way to....Hollywood

I was ready to leave after that, and it came in my mind to look up hostels. I found one in downtown Hollywood and had just enough money to get there and stay two nights. I was glad to be out of the LA bus station, but marveled how God showed up and was proud of myself for doing it. Hollywood was awesome. I felt like I was on a honeymoon with Jesus and it was exciting. I found this awesome hiking trail that overlooked the city.

That night, I walked Sunset Blvd, looking for a house of prayer that was supposed to be open. I passed by this young man who was homeless and begging for change. I didn't have money to give him, but I kneeled down in front of him and started talking. I asked him if he wanted to go to the prayer house with me. He said, "Sure." We walked a few more blocks and when we got there, it was closed!

Come on! Of all things! Instead, we went and got something to eat at a famous diner.

The company was great for the both of us and come to find out, he knew the Lord and was a really smart man, but had suffered with schizophrenia. He shared a song that he wrote that morning. It was a song God was singing over Hollywood that day: I was given similar words that same morning. Isn't it cool how God can work through a homeless man to bring blessings into the city?! Anyway, during dinner I got to pray for him with authority, prayed for him to be fully delivered. I spoke blessings over him and shared encouraging words. Most people I randomly pray for, I always wonder if there is lasting fruit. But with this man, I believe God set him free that night and he is still free. I wonder what he is doing with his life now.

The following night I got to finally meet a friend I had been introduced to over the phone the year before. He drove near my hostel and we walked Sunset Blvd, praying for and giving prophetic words to people the whole night! It was a blast! I'd say half of the people broke down in tears because they really needed to know God loved them and cared about them. It was beautiful. Others appreciated the prayer, and some looked at us like, "What just happened?" LOL.

## On My Way To....

**Roland Heights** - My friend in Redding introduced me to this amazing woman who lived outside of LA. She carries so much strength and endurance…so much hope and joy. We happened to be working in the same business and we originally met to talk about that, but after our time of meeting, she invited me to stay with her. I ended up with her for several weeks on and off, at her beautiful home at the peak of this giant mountain-ish hill, overlooking the city. She even gave me a vehicle to drive! At one point, I drove it somewhere and passed by 3 guys who were hitchhiking. Holy Spirit told me to turn around and pick them up. I did not hesitate to think if that would be a good idea or not. I just obeyed. We ended up talked about Jesus; they were from Europe, younger guys, and I introduced them to Holy Spirit.

**Santa Monica** – I met her while I was in Redding. She worked with celebrities and had a bit of a secretive life. She talked about her experiences with Christians who tried to minister to celebrities and how many of them had the wrong approach…were too hasty or tried to change them. She talked a lot about loving people and waiting on God for opportunities, not being so eager to tell them about Jesus…. even waiting years if she had too.

**Pasadena** – One of my favorite places! It was a bit calmer than LA (okay, a lot calmer), and the mountains were easily accessible and beautiful! I stayed with a house of prayer worship leader, enjoyed her company and explored the hiking trails on the mountains. Wow. That was a great time! That was when God began to ask me, "What do you want?" I was sitting on top of Echo Mountain when I tried to search out what I wanted. All I could think of was souls. I wanted people to know Jesus. But that's not what He was looking for. What do *you* want? It took a week before I felt worthy and unselfish enough to come up with something. He wanted to give me the desires of my heart. Like, personal, detailed, normal desires that He wanted to fulfill (Psalm 37:4). So cool.

### On my way to....Palm Springs

I met her at the School of Prophets training. She dressed like a rock star and had tattoos everywhere and some pretty bold makeup. It looked like people avoided her. Maybe they didn't, but I didn't want her to be left out, so I sat down next to her and started talking. She ended up being incredibly anointed and so sweet! We developed a friendship and that's how I ended up in Palm Springs with her family.

They own a makeup business and regularly pray for their customers to be healed. So, when we all came together, it was like fire! So. Much. Fun. Her husband honored and complimented me for my "style" of ministering. I just start talking to people like a normal person, and if God shows up, He shows up…if not, we had a nice conversation.    So, between that, my friend's kind heart, and the anointing for healing, we had a crazy awesome time together.

We took his 1950 money green convertible Ford Coupe out for a spin one day. I saw this man limping on the sidewalk as we drove by and said, "Pull over! That man is going to be healed today!" So, we whipped around and as we slowed down, I yelled out, "Hey we want to talk with you!" He looked a little confused or something, but as we pulled into the gas station, he came over. I smiled and approached him and we started talking. When he realized we wanted to pray for him, he put his knife away. I hadn't even *noticed* he pulled out a knife! Apparently, he just got out of jail and thought we were some gangstas that had some business with him. LOL. Ha-ha! It was the car. The gangsta car peaked his curiosity (and probably the pretty girl yelling at him). Anyway, my friends prayed for him and really touched his life. He got healed and said he wanted to recommit his life to Jesus. We took our time talking with him, and other people started gathering around us. They prayed for another woman who was totally bent over. Her back straightened up for the first time in 20 years! She was crying with so much gratitude. Then this little old man came over and cheered us on. Jesus showed up that day in the entire parking lot. It was awesome.

My friend who I met up with in Hollywood also drove down to meet up with us. We decided to go to Costco to find people to pray for. The presence and anointing of God filled the store! We prayed for one person after the next. Almost every single person we walked by, God touched. Even an entire family. Right there in the store. The presence of God came so strong that two of them almost fell over! So many people were getting healed that I walked up to the front to ask if I could make an announcement over the speakers and invite everyone in the store for prayer. But they didn't have a speaker system. Anyway, before we left we got a hot dog and pizza and realized we had better go. We had been in there for four hours!

1950 money green Ford Coupe and my friend Natalie

## On my way to....Yosemite

A friend took me to visit his friends who lived near Yosemite. They have a ministry on Friday nights with about a dozen cabins on their property for guests to come and stay for a retreat away from the busy city life. It was a beautiful place and beautiful people. It was during that time that I told them about this guy I liked, but wasn't sure if he liked me or it would ever go anywhere. They saw how much I lit up when I talked about him and encouraged me to have a conversation with him. So, I did. It was God's perfect timing because he had been talking to his friend about how much he liked me but needed a sign to let him know I had some kind of an interest in him. We officially began dating during that phone conversation. A year and a half later I became his wife! ☺

# 11

## BUSINESS

When God thrusted me from ministry into business, I suddenly realized how I had judged most of the US population instead of respected their hard work. I had a great job as a Personal Trainer for 9 years but I resented it half the time because I felt like it took away from ministry. I hated money because I equated it to time consuming jobs. Time consuming jobs that took people *away* from their families and *away* from pursuing the things of God. I also hated the false prosperity gospel. The get rich quick (manipulative) schemes. And the stress that comes from trying to get more money. I didn't place a high value on work because I had no idea what it had to do with my purpose in life or where God was at in all of it.

God took me to some extreme places, sending me to reach lost people, asking me to give it all away for Him. But I had (unknowingly) taken on this poverty mentality. In His desire to prune me of every idol and teach me to deny myself and live for Him, I began to view most anything pleasurable on this earth as bad, even sinful, and had zero value or vision for wealth building.

I remember a time when God woke me up and asked me to pray for a very wealthy, globally influential, Christian woman. I asked what to pray for, but as soon as I started asking, I knew it was more about what was in my own heart. I had assumed that she must have compromised somewhere in her walk with God in order to have the platform she has. And that's when God said, "You only see a part of her life. She is walking in obedience and I have chosen to give her this position." And then I realized that if I was judging her, there was no way that I would ever believe God for wealth in my own life…because there is no way that I am going to ever intentionally compromise my walk with God.

But if that is what God had for me…. let me say that again. *IF that is what God had for me* (financial wealth), then I wanted it. I wanted everything that Jesus died for me to have. He paid a high price for me to be forgiven, walk in freedom, and receive an inheritance. God wanted to bless Abraham and his descendants. Our heavenly Father *wants us* to prosper. What Father wants their kids living in lack? He just wanted us to serve *Him* in the blessings and share what we have with those around us.

My box got shattered once I met my husband and stepped into the business realm with him. I was growing in character and was actually getting to know a whole new side of God. I had no idea that wealth building and gaining territory were huge blessings from the Lord that He wanted me to walk in. I had no idea that money can be a weapon to defeat the works of satan. I had no idea how much bondage I was in because of my college loan debt. I had no idea how many people I could help once I had an overflow and multiple streams of income. I had no idea that I needed to think about saving and investing money for my children and children's children. I had no idea that being an honest employee or business owner made a difference in the world. I had no idea that business *was* ministry.

It's the Greek mindset that separates the physical from the spiritual. But the Hebrew mindset does not. Every aspect of life is centered upon God. It is inconceivable to put God over here and work over there. Life is a wheel with God at the center and His very life and principles flowing out onto every part of our life.

Even though God with me, it was tough. I was not used to utilizing systems and programs to help me manage my life or develop practical skills. I spent hours learning how to ship products, go through product training, market to a specific audience, and just about *live* on social media to get my business up and running. And then I began to doubt it all again. I couldn't quite figure out where God was in all of it or how I was impacting people for the gospel and even wondered if the devil had thrown this business in my lap to pull me away from the things of God...until I had a dream.

In the dream, I was taking care of my friend's Camry, but I wanted to drive this person's Corvette, if only for one day. I didn't even know the person who drove the Corvette, but they agreed to let me borrow it just for one day, and they would take the Camry. Sweet deal, no harm, so we traded. But half way through the day, I realized I hadn't got the person's contact info and had no way of getting the Camry back. My heart sunk as I knew that the Corvette was a much nicer ride, but it wasn't my friend's car. I had no way of getting her car back. About that time, this older white-haired woman appeared to me. She was friendly, humble, and it seemed that she knew me, but I didn't know her. She was trying to talk to me but I wouldn't listen because I didn't trust her. And then I woke up.

I realized that *wisdom* appeared to me like a wise older woman. She was trying to teach me, but I hadn't listened to her and sadly, didn't even recognize her. God had given me a business to steward (Camry) and that it was HIS business. I was irresponsible in my stewardship of it but secretively dreamed of living a Corvette lifestyle. I needed to learn how to take care of what God had currently put before me before I graduated to another level. When I received that revelation, I repented immediately and relief came over me. I wasn't fully sure that God had put that business in my lap and couldn't fully own it because of that. My greatest desire is to please my King, so not knowing if I was fully in His will was very troubling for me. But once I realized it was mine to steward, I got excited.

I started to own it. Like I had fun with it and didn't feel guilty about the time I spent to run it with excellence. I took responsibility to steward it well. I listened to teachings from Dani Johnson, Gary Keesee, and Dave Ramsey. If I *want an increase, I need to be faithful with the little.* Even do the budgeting. All of it. I learned new skills related about intrapersonal relationships and communication. I read books and learned to really trust my man and how God was leading him.

I learned the importance of working for something. It took time and patience! There were no cutting corners, although there were many occasions to make a few extra bucks by going against company policy (which we mostly did not do. I cannot say I followed all the rules to an exact "t" 100% of the time. But for the most part, we knew God wouldn't bless us if we broke the rules). I was developing the *character* of Christ and offering a valuable service to people. I did all those things I thought I never could do and grew in confidence. I was able to implement my own ideas and get creative with the business.

The business didn't boom just because I tithed, walked in the favor of God and prayed. Although we did well, we didn't reach the top in sales at that time. I was like, "God! How are people gonna see You in my life if my sales are not as good as the others?" He was apparently not too concerned with how many sales I could get. He just wanted my honesty and diligence. Financial wealth would come later, but I had some foundational principles to learn.

I learned what my strengths were and *were not.* I'm not great at everything. Point blank. I'm not supposed to be. That's what having a team is for. Teamwork, on the surface, was easy. But when it came down to it, I had such severe trust issues because of my past that I was a lone ranger at heart. Nothing great was achieved by a single person. It takes a team, a tribe, a family, a community, a nation…working together, to cause great things to happen. I had to learn how to trust.

I continued to grow in leadership and joined the John Maxwell Team. Speaking was a passion of mine. I originally joined to hone that skill, but it turned into a business and even a calling. I got hired to work with a small business, do leadership trainings with a college and a church, and started training people to facilitate the health course I developed in prisons. I loved empowering others to grow up in their own potential. I grew in confidence and quit telling myself lies like, "I don't know how. I can't do it. Who is going to listen to me? I am a fraud." Wow. I had a mindset that would not allow me to grow up into all that God had for me. A spirit of deception was causing me to see myself as "not good enough" in almost every area of my life. It's true that apart from God, I can accomplish *nothing* for the kingdom of God. And it's also true that "with Him, ALL things are possible." I was limiting God based on how I believed about myself. I needed to see that I was *not* the person I used to be, I had the education and skills to do the job, I was worth the money, and God was with me.

Business taught me a vital kingdom principle. It taught me the authority that God originally gave Adam and Eve; to "rule and reign." I spent many years following Christ, waiting on Him, trusting His direction. Business gave me the mindset to be like my heavenly Father and have the confidence to take the land. When you are rescued from "Egypt", God wants you to occupy "land." God doesn't just save us from hell. He brings us into what we were created to do and gives us purpose on the earth. There are places in the earth that the enemy has ruled in…areas that *you* are meant to rule in, with the authority of Jesus. Jesus broke every stronghold so that we are free to rule and reign on the earth, thereby making a way for the Lord to come and dwell amongst us (Genesis 1:28 and Isaiah 40:3). Speak the Word of God over your "land" and pray now for those God will send you to serve.

We must be intentional about claiming the land for Jesus Christ, walking in the authority that He gives us, and not tolerating the enemy. You are a priestly king. A prayer warrior who has dominion in some kind of territory on this earth, especially in your own home. You are the head and not the tail. You are above and not beneath. You are the lender and not the borrower. You are a humble queen/king and have tremendous power to shift your environment. You carry the very presence of God, have His nature, and are discovering His will for the people around you.

# 12

# MARRIAGE

I cannot recall having any desire to want to be married when I was young. Or have children. My parents are amazing and showed me a lot of love, but they just didn't have the right tools to work on their love towards one another. I suppose the animosity between them had an influence on me. It didn't look safe or fun, so why would I want *that*? Plus, society didn't place any real value on marriage. Sex? Absolutely! But commitment? Honor? Faithfulness? Not so much.

I had an identity crisis. I had written men off when I was 16 and hadn't fully recovered. I didn't want to be a woman. No, I wasn't a transgender, but I just didn't want to play the role of a "weak" woman. I didn't want to dress "pretty." I was extremely feminine but tried my best to convince myself I was tough because I didn't want to get hurt. Gentle, nurturing, caring…these were weak qualities. Stay at home mom? House wife? I saw zero value in those things. My dad, now *he* had value! He was a tough, hard-working business owner. I somehow concluded that money, education, status, and "success" gave a person value.

Discovering my identity as an adopted daughter of God and knowing my worth as a woman didn't come easily. It is a process. Part of that process included me forgiving all the men…the ones who directly hurt me, the ones who ignored me, and the ones who struggled with lust, making me feel uneasy in their presence. And forgiving myself. For all the choices I made. The evil spirits and damage that I invited into my life from what I did. And forgiving the generations of women who emasculated, manipulated, and overthrew the men in the name of "equality." What have we done? As a society. We have destroyed the beauty and uniqueness of the male and female genders. I've gone down a very difficult road and because God met me on that road, I've come to deeply appreciate and respect both men and women. I saw the value in women and difficult job that mothers have in raising children. Instead of the fear and hatred towards men, I wanted to get to know them. It's like discovering a new species on a new planet. LOL. I was in awe of God and so grateful for giving me such a love and appreciation for the men. I saw how significant their role is in the earth. And I could not wait to be married to one.

I did have great examples of marriages in the church, but it was rare. I still had a ton of negative examples, and I was still very afraid and nervous, so I was pretty serious and intentional about asking the Lord to bring me HIS best and at the right time.

I did not go on *one date* for ten years. I stayed single, not because I wanted to be single all the time, but because what else was I going to do? I was following God and if He didn't open that door, I had no business walking through it. I wouldn't have known what to do anyway. LOL. So, I stayed busy with life and waited.

I liked this one guy for a long time. We seemed like we'd be a perfect match! But he never liked me and I chalked it up to, well, that was not God's best for me. I had a lot of single girl friends who asked God to show them who their husbands were. Others dated here and there to see if one would work out. I read somewhere that in some cultures, the father would pick out the best candidate for his daughter and present him to her. She could say yes or no. I loved that idea! So, I prayed and asked my heavenly Father to pick out the best for me. He knows me so well and knows what I needed. I also liked that I had a choice in the matter and wouldn't be forced to marry someone.

It seemed like an eternity at times waiting for God to bring me my guy. For the most part, I lived a life of adventure and either enjoyed the singleness and time with Jesus, or I didn't mind it. Other times, I would find myself crawled up in a ball crying out to God to bring me someone and take away the loneliness. As I pressed into prayer, I would be able to identify my pain with other people's pains and stop feeling sorry for myself. (This happens often in my prayer life. Whatever I personally go through, God uses as an intercessory tool to pray for others. He wants me praying with my heart.

## Meeting My Hubby

Andrew and I met through a mutual friend at a Starbucks. His eyes peaked my curiosity: I could clearly see his heart. He was surprisingly transparent and honest and seemed like he could be a good friend. We prayed for this guy at the table next to us, which made me really happy. He thought I was friendly, probably friendly to all people, and left it up to me to call him if I wanted to or not. Which worked out great, because I probably would have ran had he chased after me.

We did not live in the same state, but traveled quite a bit and randomly got to meet up all over the country. It was so fun! He made me laugh more than anyone I had ever met. One summer, my cousins needed a babysitter and asked if I wanted to move into their basement and be a nanny. Wow. What a blessing. Not only was I able to spend more time with my family (and get paid), I was also able to see my guy. I also knew I was really starting to like him at that time and sensed Holy Spirit ask me not to call him to hang out. (God didn't want me to pursue him). It worked out because he ended up calling me and we would hang out every week.

We remained friends for a year before we started courting. He said I "friend-zoned" him. LOL. I did not! I just didn't flirt. At all. I still had those feelings of being a harlot and that was one thing I didn't want to feel ever again. So, if he liked me, he needed to come and get me! It was an interesting compromise on how we found out we liked each other and started dating (i.e. that phone conversation when I was in Cali).

Our first date was at Riverwalk in San Antonio, Texas; a gorgeous section of downtown San Antonio with adorable restaurants, hotels and stores right along this canal. The whole thing looked like Italy. It was so romantic! He held my hand as we were strolling along. I was a little nervous but so glad he did that: it helped us to move beyond the friend-zone. Towards the end of our walk, he looked at me in the eyes and said, "I don't believe in dating just to date. I want to court you with the intentions of marriage." Wow! I told him, "I feel the same way." We were entering into this with serious intentions yet having a blast. We also made it clear that we both wanted to stay pure until marriage.

The only curveball was….

I had no freaking idea how tough the courtship was going to be! I thought I was healed! I mean, *ten years* of inner healing and deliverance before I met the dude, so what the heck?! Apparently, God took me seriously when I told him I wanted a "solid foundation." Man, oh man! It was a whirlwind of emotions, both awesome and awful. My man struggled and worked through a lot, but didn't seem to go through the hell I went through. I think that's because he didn't have the expectations and unforgiveness like I did.

I really knew *nothing* about men. I remember being so angry at God for making us so different. Communicating with him was so freaking hard! I couldn't understand it. With my girlfriends, we just talked. Easily. Back and forth. Rarely any misunderstandings, or pauses, or keeping our feelings hidden. We just talk and talk. With this man…not the case. People say men are simple. And, yes, I do think they don't carry the complicated thinking that us women do (I have come to really appreciate that), but it was certainly not easy for me. He would completely misinterpret what I meant, what I was saying, and then wouldn't ask to understand it. He'd ignore me, get angry, or seem to not deal with it. Which caused me to press in even harder to get an answer. Anything. I don't care what it is. If you hate me, tell me. But the silence…omg it is the worst!

I finally realized that he wasn't silent in his brain. I later learned that he was, in fact, thinking through things. He cared a lot about me. He didn't want to make matters worse by saying the wrong thing, and he didn't know what to do. He had never been in a relationship where they communicated. He didn't grow up knowing how to be vulnerable and he was scared too.

Those were very difficult times for me because the feelings of neglect triggered some major wounds from my past. There were other patterns between us that exposed low self-worth and rejection in me. I interpreted his actions as: "I don't care enough about you to even try to meet you where you are at. You're not worth it. You don't matter. You aren't valuable." But that's not at all what he thought or said. I was unaware at how much of a victim I was. And afraid. And co-dependent. That fear gave the devil permission to torment me. Not only was I dealing with relational issues, I had demons swarming around me. I know there were Psalm 91 angels, but I relied on my feelings more than what I knew to be true and gave in to the fear.

Any normal person would have left the relationship if it was causing that many problems. But I kept praying. I was willing to stay. I was willing to leave. God, just show me Your will and what is best for me! Over and over, God said, "Trust Me" and told me that He wanted to produce *love* in our relationship. He was working all things together to produce love. I had friends I had asked to council me - prayer warriors who never once cautioned me or suggested that I leave. They all felt peaceful about us being together. So, I kept seeking the Lord and reading the Word and my guy and I did our best to communicate.

I wasn't alone; Andrew was praying too. We were given insight and discernment to see what the enemy was up to. There was a battle raging and we needed to fight the enemy, not fight against each other. We flew out to Oregon for a week of healing and deliverance. And hired a professional therapist. We grew stronger and became best friends and continued to have a blast together, in spite of the intense struggles at times. If you know my guy, you know he can't be serious for too long. His humor saved us from the heaviness. ☺

While visiting friend in Texas, Abba woke me up one morning at 6am and said, "I want to give you away in marriage." The Lord comforted my heart and prepared me ahead of time. It was such a sweet moment between the Lord and I.

Andrew had asked for my dad's blessing months prior. I was impatiently waiting for him to ask me, thinking he wasn't planning anything, but he sure was! He paid off my ring so it would be 100%

mine when I got it. He took me to Eagle Mountain Park and asked me to bring my bible. We hiked down the well-manicured walkway where the yellow cactus flowers were blooming and we ended up overlooking a lake. I stood on this giant rock and began to read Isaiah 34 about how the "Spirit of the Lord has gathered them and not one shall lack a mate." Ha-ha! Can you believe I just "happened" to read that?! I was so excited reading that scripture that he almost didn't want to ruin the moment. LOL. But he started to pray and then got down on one knee to ask me to marry him and for a split-second fear almost tried to come, but I remembered that morning with the Lord and was certain that this man I loved dearly was God's will. Before he got all the words out, I screamed, "Yes Yes Yes!!!"

My former pastor and his wife and six children traveled over 1,000 miles to perform our ceremony. Literally, every one of them except for the baby was in our wedding. I just love them. They all either spoke, read scripture, or sang. I loved it. I didn't want something too religious feeling and thought asking the kids to join was perfect. Plus, it never made sense to me why one man would marry a couple. Hello! Shouldn't a married couple do the ceremony and speak a blessing over us? LOL. That was just me, and Andrew, being the amazing man he is, laughed and agreed with me.

I am so grateful God was in our midst and kept us together. It was so worth it! My husband is amazing. He has a great sense of humor and brought the intensity down many times. He is incredibly forgiving and has so much grace for me. He was willing to work on his part and grow, even though it seemed SO. MUCH. SLOWER. Than my pace. And definitely in *his* way, not mine. I learned that the hard way – he refuses to be controlled. LOL. He is courageous, steadfast, and unmovable. A great provider and my best friend. Had I listened to the devil and my own flesh, I would have missed out on the second greatest gift I could have ever received in life.

One other surprise blessing: I lived in Florida my whole life, but my husband lives in the same state...the same city as the rest of my family! I moved into his house with him. Never in my life did I think that would happen! Our first year of marriage, I was able to visit my grandparents every week and get to know them even more. I got to see my grandpa every day for the last week of his life. And, God answered our prayers. My grandma led him to the Lord just one week before he died. Incredible.

## Power Struggle

This is probably obvious, but marriage doesn't work out too well if both people are fighting to be right or in control. I haven't been married long enough to do any kind of marriage seminar or even write a book on it, but I will just share what I've learned thus far. We are equal. Equal in ability, worth, power, and intellect. We are equally loved and respected. My voice matters, it gets to be heard. His voice matters. Sometimes I need to shut my mouth and sometimes he gets to listen. While we are equal, I do believe that the man is a leader and head of his home. It is not about him being better than me; it's about design and position. God designed the puzzle pieces to fit together a certain way. I know Andrew is a great leader because when he makes decisions, (most of the time) he is thinking about what is best for our family, not just what is best for himself. Trust is necessary. Not merely in the man, but in God. Chaos happens when there is no trust and there isn't divine order. Just ask any military officer what their soldiers are like when there is no respect or commander in charge. I also believe that women have a unique role in intercessory prayer. Men pray too. They must if they want to lead the family in God's will. But wives and moms seem to have an important role in keeping the devil out of the family. I found that the devil would often attack me in order to get to my husband. He would whisper accusations against my man that would cause division. He was trying to take him down and ultimately our marriage down through me! On many occasions I had revelatory insight into the schemes of the devil. But many times, I failed and began to attack my husband. Eventually, I overcame and gained ground and quit allowing the devil to dupe me into another fight (of course my husband needed to learn this too, and he did). The battle is never against my husband. The battle is against wicked forces, as Ephesians 6 says.

Marriage is worth fighting for. It's so hard at times, but so worth it. It is more than a contract: it's a covenant. A covenant is unconditional and deep; sacred.

*Friend, if you are struggling in your marriage, don't compare yours to anyone else's. No one has a perfect marriage. There is only one who is perfect and His name is God. I encourage you to not blame your spouse or your parents. Put down the weapons of defense, anger, bitterness, jealousy, and strife. Keep sitting at the feet of Jesus. Allow Him to wrap His arms around you and show you His love and His ways. Death to self is a very real calling that He calls all of us to. Most don't want to die to themselves and truly live unto the Lord. (It's hard! Shoot. So many times, I fight it. I don't want to lay down my rights and demands.) But it's worth it. The reward for following Jesus is greater than we could ever imagine. And, if you are in an abusive relationship, seek counsel immediately. There is a time to speak up and say, "No" and set strong boundaries. Ask God for wisdom and seek wise council.*

# *13*

# *A Baker's Dozen*

Last year I invested in an intense emotional intelligence and leadership training with a secular organization. The world has great principles in leadership and prosperity, sometimes more so than the church. It blew my mind. I didn't even know anything like that existed. God used it to grow me in areas where I was stuck. And in other areas that I didn't even know needed to be grown.

For example, I had no idea that I thought of unbelievers as an outreach project. (Where is one of those oops emoji's when you need one?). All of my friends were strong believers. I loved people and wanted them to know Jesus, but because of my new lifestyle, I just didn't hang out with unbelievers unless it was at an AA meeting or in the workplace. All those relationships stayed on a surface level. My tribe were tongue talking, miracle working prayer machines. And, I think that was fine. God wanted to work the world out of me and renew my mind. But I didn't know how much I had segregated myself out of fear.     I was afraid to get too close to unbelievers because I was scared I'd end up compromising my values and walk away from Jesus. Not totally walk away, but live like a lukewarm Christian. I was afraid that I would start to think and act like an unbeliever. I was afraid that the demons I was just delivered from would someone jump right back onto me. I was afraid that I would lose my zeal for God. I knew I was weak and prone to wander after the shiny things of the world.    Listen, any time we are walking in fear, we are not walking in love. I thought it was wise to not get too close to unbelievers, and, to an extent, that can be true. But I wasn't acting with the motivation of wisdom, I was reacting with my old protective friend fear. The more I got to know the people in that organization (namely the unbelievers), the more embarrassed I became. I was so taken back at how well they had succeeded in so many things. How well they were doing in their careers, how well they responded in love and gentleness. All I could think of was, "God, they act more like Jesus than I do! How are you going to be glorified in my life when their results are better than mine? Their everything seems to be better. They play team better than me. They are more organized than me. I love you the most.  I am the one who is supposed to shine the light and love of Christ and I feel so hidden, so average, so below average. How are you going to be glorified in my life?" Every bit of that pride and performance driven mentality rose up in me. I based my value and ability to be an effective witness on external results. It's true that God is glorified by the fruit in our life and the actions steps we take in obedience to Him, but I based it all on ME and what I could do instead of letting the focus be on HIM and what He can do. One of the greatest things I learned was to just get to know people. Everyone has a story. Before you decide you think you know what they need to do, get to know them! You do not know what people need to do or not do. Only God knows their hearts. He knows the pain they've walked through, their experiences that have shaped the way they think, their desires, their insecurities. People are people. It's not our job to convert. It's our job to love well and always be listening to Holy Spirit. I hope I did an okay job at wrapping up each chapter because I do not have a way to wrap up this book. LOL. Perhaps someday I will make each chapter into a book. A friend and mentor made that suggestion to me one day; it seemed like a "God idea." But since I can't just end this book here, I'll leave you with a prayer that I'd like to pray for you...

*Lord, life can be such a mystery. You give and take away, like the song goes, but my heart will choose to say, Thank You Lord. I pray right now for this person who is reading this book. I pray for you. That you would know the hope of your calling in Christ. That you would swat away the demons that have influenced your thinking and life...swat them away as easily as a cow swats gnats with its tail. LOL. It doesn't even stop chewing the grass to look up; it just swats away. I pray that you would walk in that authority on behalf of your close family members, your co-workers, your employees, your city, your nation. I pray that you would have dreams, visions, impressions, and an internal knowing of who God is. I pray that you would choose to take the time that is required to walk in the Holy Spirit. It is very easy to use our natural minds to navigate through life. We are capable of much apart from God, which is scary. But nothing we do without Him will mean anything in eternity. My coach was once asked, "Who is all of this for?" I pray you will continually evaluate your motivations and why you are doing what you are doing. Who is it for? If it's for Jesus, then you will find peace and clarity in knowing what His will is and what direction to go in. And don't forget, it's not about doing His will, it's about growing in your relationship with Him over time, which will result in some really great things. Not without trials and hardship though, so don't be sold into thinking life is supposed to be easy if you follow God. Sometimes it's harder. But we have the divine Helper who is ready to help you every step of the way. Be blessed.*

# REFERENCES

Holy Bible Ghana Student Edition, Tyndale House Publishers, Inc. New Living Translation, Second Edition.

www.ingramcontent.com/pod-product-compliance
Lightning Source LLC
Chambersburg PA
CBHW021210020426
42331CB00003B/286